games handbook

OUTDOOR GAMES!

Lisa Regan

QED Publishing

Editor: Sarah Eason
Designer: Calcium
Illustrators: Owen Rimington and Emma DeBanks

Copyright © QED Publishing 2010

First published in the UK in 2010 by
QED Publishing
A Quarto Group company
226 City Road
London EC1V 2TT

www.qed-publishing.co.uk

A catalogue record for this book is available
from the British Library.

ISBN 978 1 84835 360 2

Printed in China

CONTENTS

HOW TO USE THIS BOOK

Let's play outside – here comes the sun, the perfect place to have some fun!

So, you are outside with space to run and to play whatever you like. Whether you are in the park, at the beach, in your own garden or even in the school playground, there are some great games here to try. Make the most of running free and getting some fresh air and exercise – it's play time!

You will need

Many of the games in this book just need you and a few friends. Some of them need a ball, and a few suggest you use beach toys, garden toys or things you find around you, such as sticks and stones. There are also rules for games with special equipment, such as marbles – read through the book and take your pick.

Players

Lots of outdoor games were invented in the playground, where you have a big group of friends to play with. Some of the games in this book are good fun for a small group of players. If no one wants to play, read the 'On your own?' feature to see how to adapt the game to play by yourself.

4

Difficulty

No one wants to waste time playing outdoor games with lots of complicated rules, so all these games are quite easy. You will need to practise some games before you get really good at them. The easiest games are marked with * and are at the beginning of the book. The hardest games are at the end, marked * * * * *, and the games in between are – well, in between!

STEPPING STONES

Carefully move your box each time, and head towards the finish line.

Difficulty: ★★★ Players: 2 or more

You will need:
- two shoe boxes per player

1 This is a racing game. Play against the other players, or make two teams for a relay race.

2 Use your boxes as stepping stones. Put the first one down (with the open side facing up) and step into it. Put the second box in front and place your other foot inside.

3 Lift your back foot and move the empty box forwards. Keep going until you reach the end. If it's a relay race, run back to the start and pass the boxes to the next player.

On Your Own?
Use a stopwatch to record how fast you can race from one end of the garden to the other.

Bet You Can't!
Make a rule that you must return to the start if your foot touches the ground.

The winner is... the first team or person to reach the finish line – without collapsing in a heap or breaking their boxes!

20

RIVER MONSTER

Aagh! Don't let the monster get you, but cross the river if it lets you.

Difficulty: ★★★ Players: 3 or more

You will need:
- skipping rope or string

1 Mark out the banks of a 'river' using skipping ropes, string or lines drawn in the sand.

2 Two players stand in the river and form the 'monster' by linking arms. The other players have to run across the river as the monster tries to catch them.

3 Anyone who is caught joins arms and makes the monster longer. The monster cannot leave the river with any part of its body. It becomes harder to get away as the monster grows longer!

On Your Own?
Mark out the river banks and see if you can leap across without 'falling in'. How wide can you leap?

Did You Know?
Don't try to play this game on the Amazon River in South America. Where it flows through Brazil, it is between 6 and 10 kilometres wide!

The winner is... the last person to be caught.

21

Bet You Can't!

Are you too good already? Beaten all your friends and smashed the world record? Then read this section for an extra challenging twist to put your skills to the test. Now let's see how good you are!

Did You Know?

For some games you will find fascinating facts related to them, to add to the fun.

5

BALLOON BASH

Throw your balloons up into the air. Hit them, though you can't see where!

Difficulty: **Players:** 2 or more

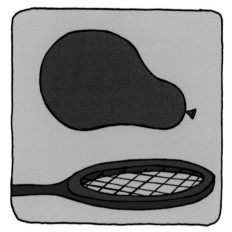

1 Take it in turns to cover your eyes with a scarf (carefully), so that you cannot see the balloons. The other players can stop you from tripping or bumping into things.

2 Throw the balloons gently up into the air. Use a tennis racquet or a rolled-up newspaper to try to hit a balloon.

3 Score a point for every time you make a hit. You'll be able to feel it, and the non-blindfolded players can keep count as well.

On Your Own?

Use a long piece of string to tie a balloon to a tree or fence, and hit the balloon by yourself. If you don't move too far, you won't hurt yourself.

The winner is... the first to get ten points.

STOMP!

Jump around and stamp and hop, but don't let your balloon go pop!

Difficulty: **Players:** any number

1 Tie a balloon to the ankle of each player. Use up to a metre of thread for each one, so the balloons float away a little.

2 When someone says, "Go!" you must run and jump around, trying to burst the balloons tied to other players.

3 Make sure you keep an eye on your own balloon, as others will be out to get it!

The winner is...
the last person to have a blown-up balloon on their string.

Did You Know?

Don't play this game with British TV star Dermot O'Leary. In 2008, he held the world 'balloon popping' record – he burst 100 balloons in 25 seconds!

On Your Own?

Use a longer piece of string and run around in all directions, trying to jump on your own balloon!

MATCHBOX MAGPIES

Collect the treasures you can see, just like a magpie in a tree.

Difficulty: **Players:** any number

3 Keep checking that your box closes with all your things in it. Do not pick flowers or pick up rubbish. Do not disturb animal homes, such as birds' nests.

1 This game is easy, and can take as long as you like. Start by giving each player an empty matchbox.

2 Hunt around your outdoor space looking for tiny things. The aim is to fit as many different items in your box as possible.

The winner is...
the person who collects the greatest number of different things.

On Your Own?
This is great fun for one player – but don't wander off too far from a grown-up.

Bet You Can't!
List three items that everyone HAS to find, such as a petal, a blade of grass and a wood chipping.

POOH STICKS

Throw your stick and watch it flow – everyone can have a go!

Difficulty: **Players:** 2 or more

You will need:
....
• small sticks

Don't play this game without having an adult to supervise you.

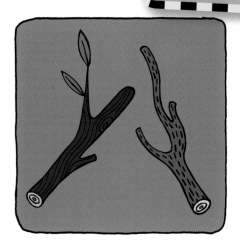

1 You have to play this game standing on a bridge over a stream. Be careful! Make sure you stand upstream, so the water is flowing under the bridge behind you.

2 Each player chooses a stick. Try to pick one that looks different from the others, so that you can recognize which one is yours.

3 Drop the sticks into the stream all at the same time, then run to the other side of the bridge, and wait…

Did You Know?

This game is named after Winnie the Pooh, the bear who plays it with Christopher Robin in the stories by A.A. Milne.

The winner is... the person whose stick appears first from under the bridge.

9

STAR WARS

You will need:
....
- just your feet!

Don't step on cracks seen in the street – a game for people with small feet!

Difficulty: **Players:** any number

1 Here's a game to play walking down a street. It's good fun on a long shopping trip.

On Your Own?

This is easy peasy to play alone – but harder if you are in a hurry!

2 As you walk along the pavement, try not to step on the cracks between the paving stones.

3 Carefully place your feet so they are totally inside each paving stone. Anyone who steps on a crack goes over to the Dark Side of the Force!

Bet You Can't!
See if you are skilled enough to play on tiny stones. You have to tiptoe! That's why Darth Vader is on the dark side – his feet are too big!

The winner is...
anyone who stays off the cracks. You can play with grown-ups, even if they don't know they are playing!

GIANT'S SHOES

Fee-fi-fo-fum,
who will be the fastest in this run?

Difficulty: **Players:** 2 players or 2 equal teams

You will need:
....
- two pairs of BIG shoes
- skipping rope or string
- chalk

3 If you are playing in teams, take off the shoes so that the next team member can race in them.

1 Make a starting line and a finish line. Use skipping ropes or string, or draw a line with chalk. Put a pair of giant shoes on the starting line for each player or team.

2 When someone says, "Go!" Put on the shoes, and carefully race towards the finish line. Turn around and run back to the starting line.

The winner is...

the person, or team, that finishes first. Anyone who loses a shoe must put it on again before they can continue running.

On Your Own?

Make an obstacle course and run around it wearing your giant's shoes.

Bet You Can't!

Make the game harder by running sideways, or even backwards. If you're just too good for this game, turn it into an egg-and-spoon race using bouncy balls and spoons.

11

MR WOLF

Slowly creep to Wolfman's line, but run when he shouts, "Dinner time!"

Difficulty: **Players:** any number

1 One player is Mr Wolf. He stands a few metres away from the others, with his back turned. The players stand in a row and shout, "What time is it, Mr Wolf?"

2 Mr Wolf answers, "Three o'clock!" and the players creep forwards three steps. Each time they ask, he can say a different time. If Mr Wolf turns round, the players must freeze.

3 If Mr Wolf shouts "Dinner time!", or if a player gets near enough to touch Mr Wolf, he chases everyone back to the starting line.

Bet You Can't!
Make the game more fun on a warm day by giving Mr Wolf a watering can. Anyone he catches gets sprinkled!

The winner is...
anyone who gets safely back to the start. If Mr Wolf catches someone, that person becomes Mr Wolf.

On Your Own?
Practise creeping up on a chosen place, such as a tree – if you hear a noise, such as a siren, a bus or even birdsong, you must freeze.

12

SPLASH!

Play this on a sunny day,
to wash your cobwebs clean away!

Difficulty: **Players:** 2 or more

You will need:
....
• water bomb balloons

1 This game is very easy, but SO splashy! Fill a water bomb balloon so that it is quite full, and tie the end.

2 Throw the water bomb from player to player. Be careful not to drop it, or you'll get wet!

3 Be careful, too, how you catch it. It's easy to burst a water bomb just by closing your hands around it!

Bet You Can't!
Play over a washing line or tennis net. The throws will have to be bold, so everyone will have to be on their guard!

On Your Own?
See how brave you can be – throw the water bomb higher each time, and make sure you catch it!

The winner is...
there is no winner – just a lot of wet players, usually!

FINDERS KEEPERS

You will need:
....
- pencils
- paper
- coins

Play this game of treasure seekers.
Look for money – finders keepers!

Difficulty: **Players:** any number

1 Each player writes a list of things to find. It can include nature items (such as leaves or seeds) or toys, but not pieces of litter. The choice will vary if you are at the park, the garden or the beach.

2 Swap your list with another player. Set a time limit for each player to collect as many listed items as they can.

3 For an added bonus, write 'coin' on the lists and ask a grown-up to hide small change nearby.

The winner is...
the person who collects the most things from their list. Remember not to stray too far.

On Your Own?
Find your own things, or ask a grown-up to make a list for you.

Did You Know?
Dandelion plants get their name from the French *dent de lion*, which means 'lion's tooth'.

CRAZY GOLF

Crazy golf is so much fun – can you score a hole in one?

Difficulty: **Players:** any number

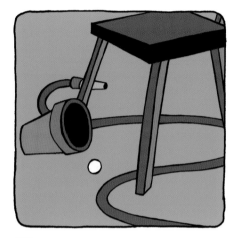

1 Set up your own crazy golf course, using anything you can find as obstacles. If you are at the beach, dig holes in the sand and build walls and tunnels.

2 If you are in the garden, use plant pots on their side for the holes, and make a course with the hosepipe, round a swing, under a bench… make it as difficult as you like.

3 Use a ball and a stick, or a mini golf set, to play a ball around the course.

The winner is... the person who uses the least number of shots to finish – but half the fun is setting up the crazy course!

On Your Own?

Not a problem – you can play this by yourself for hours.

Did You Know?

Mini-golf is played semi-professionally by some people, and you can watch it on TV sports channels. It is possible to win over £50,000 as prize money, so get practising!

WORKS OF ART

Pile your stones up, nice and tall.
Be careful you don't let them fall!

Difficulty: **Players:** any number

1 Each player collects a heap of pebbles, stones and small rocks. Find a flat surface to work on.

3 Experiment with different designs, or just try to make the tallest tower you can!

You will need:
• pebbles
• stones
• rocks

On Your Own?
This game is great to pass time alone, and you can really concentrate on what you're doing.

2 The idea is simple – pile up the stones, starting with the largest at the bottom, to make a sculpture.

The winner is...
the person with the highest sculpture, or the most artistic or the best balanced... you decide.

Did You Know?
Rock balancing is recognized as art, and has been made famous by artists such as Bill Dan in the United States and Andy Goldsworthy in the UK.

OLYMPIC RINGS

You will need:
....
• hula hoops or other rings

Do your friends say you're acting loopy? Tell them you're just hula hoopy!

Difficulty: **Players:** any number

1 There are lots of games to play with rings and hoops. Try standing a few metres away from a target, such as a bucket or a small chair. See if you can throw your hoop to land over the target.

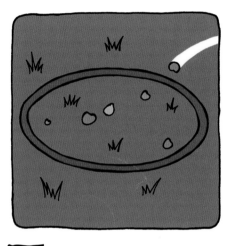

2 Hoop rolling is harder than it looks. Can you roll your hoop, on its side, so that it goes between two goalposts?

3 Place the hoop on the floor and stand well back. Try to throw stones or balls so they land inside the hoop, without touching the edges.

Did You Know?

Historians have found that people played games with hoops (made of woven grass or sticks) thousands of years ago in ancient Egypt.

On Your Own?

Not a problem – practise all the events alone and try to beat your own best scores.

The winner is...

the person who wins the most events in your own hula Olympics.

FROG HOPPERS

**Leap onto a lily pad,
to make that heron hopping mad!**

Difficulty: **Players:** the more the better

2 The players run around until a grown-up shouts out "Here comes the heron!" Everyone has to hop onto a lily pad to stay safe.

3 When the grown-up says "Hmm, nothing to eat today", everyone runs around again. Take away one of the lily pads each time, so that it becomes harder to find a safe place.

1 Place single sheets of newspaper all around your playing area, but not touching each other. These are your 'lily pads'.

On Your Own?
Leap from one lily pad to another, making the gaps between them bigger each time.

The winner is... the last 'frog' on the last lily pad.

Did You Know?
The largest heron in the United States, the great blue heron, eats frogs but it also gobbles down lizards, snakes, muskrats, prairie dogs and baby alligators!

BOULES

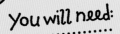

Here's a game of care and skill, winning gives you such a thrill!

Difficulty: ⭐⭐⭐ **Players:** 2 or more

You will need:
....
- one small ball or stone
- two bigger balls or stones per player

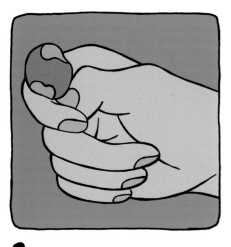

1 One player throws the small ball or stone across the play area. Try to throw it about 5 metres. This is the 'jack'.

2 Each player throws their first ball or stone, trying to make it land as close to the jack as possible. If you are using stones, choose ones that are different from each other so you can tell which are yours.

3 The players then take their second throw. Aim to land closest to the jack, or to knock any of the other balls or stones out of the way.

On Your Own?

This game is addictive and you can spend ages practising on your own to get really good.

Bet You Can't!

Hit the jack and knock it out of the way of the other players' balls.

The winner is...

the person whose ball or stone is closest to the jack.

19

STEPPING STONES

Carefully move your box each time, and head towards the finish line.

Difficulty: ⭐⭐⭐ **Players:** 2 or more

You will need:
....
• two shoe boxes per player

1 This is a racing game. Play against the other players, or make two teams for a relay race.

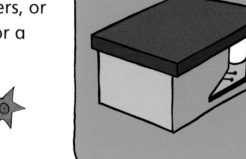

On Your Own?

Use a stopwatch to record how fast you can race from one end of the garden to the other.

2 Use your boxes as stepping stones. Put the first one down (with the open side facing up) and step into it. Put the second box in front and place your other foot inside.

3 Lift your back foot and move the empty box forwards. Keep going until you reach the end. If it's a relay race, run back to the start and pass the boxes to the next player.

Bet You Can't!
Make a rule that you must return to the start if your foot touches the ground.

The winner is...
the first team or person to reach the finish line – without collapsing in a heap or breaking their boxes!

20

RIVER MONSTER

Aagh! Don't let the monster get you, but cross the river if it lets you.

Difficulty:  **Players:** 3 or more

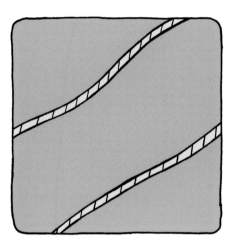

1 Mark out the banks of a 'river' using skipping ropes, string or lines drawn in the sand.

2 Two players stand in the river and form the 'monster' by linking arms. The other players have to run across the river as the monster tries to catch them.

3 Anyone who is caught joins arms and makes the monster longer. The monster cannot leave the river with any part of its body. It becomes harder to get away as the monster grows longer!

The winner is... the last person to be caught.

On Your Own?
Mark out the river banks and see if you can leap across without 'falling in'. How wide can you leap?

Did You Know?
Don't try to play this game on the Amazon River in South America. Where it flows through Brazil, it is between 6 and 10 kilometres wide!

21

IN THE MONEY

Water, water, everywhere.
If you win the money, will you share?

Difficulty: ⭐⭐⭐ **Players:** any number

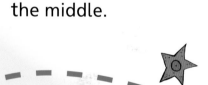

1 Put the large silver coin in the bucket of water, roughly in the middle.

2 Take it in turns to drop a copper coin into the water and see if it lands on, or partly on, the silver coin.

3 Try holding your copper coin higher or lower before you drop it. It is hard to hit the silver coin, as the water makes the falling coins move in unexpected directions.

The winner is... the person whose coin lands closest to the silver one. They might even get to keep it!

Did You Know?
In Russia in 1940, hundreds of coins fell from the sky one day. A money chest had been lifted up by a great wind called a tornado, and the coins fell out – as if someone in the heavens was playing this game!

On Your Own?
This game is just as frustrating when you play alone!

SILLY OLYMPICS

See if you can be the best.
Win your races – beat the rest.

Difficulty: ⭐⭐⭐ **Players:** any number

1 Hold your own Olympic Games with a selection of mad races. Mark out a start and finish line, and decide how many events you want to include.

Bet You Can't!
Do the same races over a homemade obstacle course.

2 Try to vary the skills you need. Balancing events could be running while carrying a ball on a spade (a bit like egg and spoon), keeping a balloon balanced on your forehead as you run or crawling with a bucket of water on your back.

3 Silly running races could be running backwards, a three-legged race, running with a ball held between your knees, or dribbling a balloon without letting it touch the ground.

On Your Own?
You might feel silly but these games are great on your own.

The winner is...
probably quite daft and also out of breath!

OFF THE WALL

Throw your stone against a wall.
The skill is where you make it fall.

Difficulty: ⭐⭐⭐ **Players:** any number

1 Each player finds a pebble they can recognize as their own. Look for different colours and shapes.

2 Take turns to throw your pebble against the wall. It will bounce back and land on the ground (as stones do).

3 The aim is to get your stone to fall close to the wall, instead of bouncing back and landing far out. It's tricky!

The winner is... the person whose stone is nearest the bottom of the wall.

Did You Know?

One of the world's biggest rocks is Uluru, in Australia. Don't try to play this game with it – it's over 800 metres high and nearly 10 kilometres around its edge.

On Your Own?

You can spend ages perfecting your skills.

24

SHARP SHOOTERS

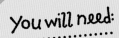

Try to be the marble king
by knocking others from the ring.

Difficulty:  **Players:** any number

You will need:
· lots of large and small marbles
· chalk

1 Draw a large circle on the ground. Draw in the dirt or sand, or use chalk. Each player puts ten small marbles in the middle of the circle.

2 Take turns to stand half a metre away, and roll or throw a larger marble into the circle, aiming for the other marbles.

3 Score a point for any marbles that are knocked outside the circle. If your large marble rolls out of the circle, you can have another go from where it landed.

Bet You Can't!
Sometimes this game is played 'for keeps' – any marbles you knock out are yours to keep. Everyone must agree that they are happy to play this way.

On Your Own?
Take three turns and add up your score. Can you beat it with another three turns?

The winner is...
the person who scores the most points.

25

SLAM!

Show your skills off with a ball, do some tricks against the wall.

Difficulty: ★ ★ ★ ★   **Players:** any number

You will need:
....
• ball (any kind)
• wall

3 Sounds easy? Now try some tricks – such as clapping, spinning around or touching the ground between throwing and catching the ball. You have to be quick!

1 Find a high wall, such as the side of a building. Stand a little way back, then throw the ball so that it bounces on the ground and then hits the wall.

2 As the ball comes back off the wall, you must try to catch it.

The winner is... the person who can do the best tricks.

Bet You Can't!
Touch the ground, do a star jump and clap behind your back before catching the ball.

On Your Own?
No problem, you can easily play by yourself and try harder tricks each time.

26

BEACH HUT

**Wait until you hear your name,
then run like crazy in this game!**

Difficulty: ★★★★ **Players:** as many as possible

You will need:
....
• just the players

2 Each player is named after an item found at the beach, such as a shell or a towel. One player makes up a story about a trip to the beach.

1 Players sit opposite each other, with their legs out straight and feet touching.

On Your Own?
Make up a story using all the things you can see around you at the beach.

3 If you hear your item mentioned in the story, you must stand up and race to the end of the row, stepping in between the legs. Then run back around the outside, and up through the middle, to sit in your place again.

Did You Know?
Sandwiches are not named after the sand you get in them at the beach. They are named after an Englishman, the Earl of Sandwich, who liked them because they were easy to eat without a knife and fork.

The winner is...
no one, but the game goes crazy when more than one player is racing around.

27

HOPSCOTCH

**Throw your stone and take a leap.
Try not to end up in a heap!**

Difficulty:  **Players:** any number

1 Copy the picture here to draw a hopscotch course on the ground. Use chalk, or if you're at the seaside, draw the lines and numbers in the sand.

2 Stand behind the first square and throw the stone so that it lands in the number 1 square, without touching the sides.

3 Now for the hopping. Hop over square 1 onto square 2, then square 3. Jump onto 4 and 5 with one foot in each. Hop onto 6, jump onto 7 and 8, and then jump right round to face back towards the start.

Did You Know?

There is a French version of this game that is played on a spiral-shaped court. It is called *escargot* which means 'snail', because of the shell shape of the court.

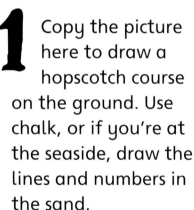

4 Hop and jump back to square 2. Bend over, balancing on one leg, and pick up the stone, then hop back to the start.

5 Now try to throw the stone into every other square in turn. Repeat the hopping and jumping, so that you do not land on the square with the stone in it. Each time you return, bend over and collect the stone.

6 It is the next person's turn if you fall, land on the square with the stone in it or miss the square when you throw the stone. Start at the number you failed on when it's your turn again.

The winner is...
anyone who manages to complete all the squares without a mistake.

On Your Own?
Play in the same way, but if you fail go back to square 1 and start again.

29

PIRATE SHIP

Pretend you're on a pirate ship, this fast-paced game will keep you fit.

Difficulty: ⭐⭐⭐⭐ **Players:** as many as possible

2 As the caller shouts instructions, all the players must follow orders as quickly as possible – but without making any mistakes.

3 The instructions all have an action – these are listed on the page opposite. Anyone who gets it wrong is out of the game. The caller can try to confuse everyone by shouting lots of instructions straight after each other.

1 One person stands at the side and calls out the instructions. The other players start in the middle of the playing area.

The winner is... the last person standing!

Did You Know?
Pirates believed that whistling on board ship would cause a storm – so there is nothing in this game that mentions whistling!

Instructions

Port
Run to the left of the playing area.

Starboard
Run to the right of the playing area.

Bow of the ship
Run to the front of the playing area.

Stern of the ship
Run to the back of the playing area.

Scrub the decks
Kneel on the ground and pretend to clean it.

Captain's coming
Stand up straight and salute.

Man overboard
Put your hand by your eyebrows as if you are looking for something.

Climb the rigging
Move your arms and legs as if you're climbing a ladder.

Ship's cat
Meow and use your hand to wash your whiskers.

Storm at sea
Stagger backwards as if you are going to fall overboard.

On Your Own?

Act out your own pirate adventure, using these instructions and any other piratey things you can think of.

TWO BALL

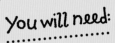

So you think you're good at catch?
This game will show you've met your match.

You will need:
....
• two balls
• wall

Difficulty: ★★★★★ **Players:** any number

  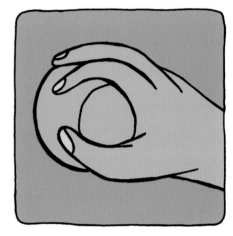

1 This game is a bit like juggling, but you play against a wall. Throw your first ball so that it comes straight back at you without bouncing on the floor.

2 Before you catch the first ball, throw the second ball at the wall in the same way.

3 Catch the first ball and throw it straight back, in time to catch the second ball. Keep going!

On Your Own?
This game is just as good if you are the only player.

The winner is...
the player who can keep going the longest without dropping either ball.